COOKIE CRUMBS

Vol. 1

By Sylvia Florence Cook Bright

COOKIE CRUMBS

CRUMBS Vol. I

By Sylvia Florence Cook Bright

Knoxville, Tennessee, USA
crippledbeaglepublishing.com

Cover Artwork: Mary Helen Gilmore Owen
Book Design: Ariane Mae A. Hipolito
Interior Artwork: Cheryl Chandler

Hardcover ISBN: 978-1-965334-40-9

Printed in the United States of America

This compulsion to write poetry began when I was in the fourth grade at South Harriman Grammar School in Roane County, Tennessee. I call it a compulsion because it seems that when the ideas, the themes, and the rhyming words start cluttering my thoughts, I must write.

There were several pieces of "Depression Glass" dishes, including a cookie jar, on the kitchen table at the home of my grandmother, Florence DeArmond Cook. As a teenager nicknamed "Cookie," I spent many delightful weekends with her. The cover of this book pays tribute to that time in my life.

CONTENTS

ADVERBIALS

Reluctantly
I admit that time and distance take their toll;
And I chafe under the burden of circumstances beyond our control.

Tenaciously
I am clinging to the thread that runs so true;
For having shared in friendship, I feel bound inseparably to you.

Emphatically
I deny that things will never be the same.
You're my friend and I'll still smile when I see your name.

Stalwartly
I defend my right to muse and reminisce.
I'll think what I want to think and miss whom I want to miss.

Sylvia Cook Bright
Copyright 1985

AT THE SALT MARSH

At the salt marsh,
In this tidal pool,
My species can thrive.
Home here is harsh;
Once warm and then cool,
And yet we survive.

My friend, The Sea,
Brings gifts, saline baths,
By her faithful tide.
Wastes wash from me
Down water-worn paths,
Now narrow, then wide.

My friend, Marine,
Storms, stirring up spume,
And crowning my reeds,
Feeds the red-green-
Brown planktonic bloom.
First fullness, then needs...

Estuarine,
Both barren and rife,
I wait for My Friend,
Who comes with brine,
With moisture with life,
On whom I depend.

Sylvia Cook Bright
Copyright 1985

BACK TO SCHOOL

Instead of standing, waiting at the door,
She straightens that third row of desks just once more,
Then checks the erasers, the chalk and the paints,
And fondly remembers last year's kindergarten saints.

The alphabet cards are taped to the wall,
And big number Ones are marked on the ball.
Meanwhile, the buses are disgorging their loads
Of lunchboxes, Barbies, Darth Vaders, and toads.

She hears the assault of sneakers on tile
And greets upturned faces with a generous smile.
She's all butterflies, though she tries to act cool.
It's the first-grade teacher's first day back to school.

Sylvia Cook Bright
Copyright 1980

CAST ALL YOUR CARE ON HIM
First Peter 5:7

"Cast all your care on Him, for He cares for you."
This is a solemn assurance; it's the best that God can do.

He wants you always to cast all your care on Him,
For He cares for you, for your every concern and whim.

Here's a bold Bible statement that surely proves to be true:
"Cast all your care on Him, for He cares for you."

Sylvia Cook Bright
Copyright 1981

CONTENTMENT

Sturdy Angus steers
Munching through the summer hayfield,
Showing only black, sleek backs
In the tall grass as they chew
Their way from one clump to another-
Theirs couldn't equal the satisfaction
That I feel with you.

Lazy old tomcat
Stretched out on the windowsill,
Occasionally mustering enough energy
To unsheathe one claw, maybe two,
Only to curl them back in again-
Yet he's not nearly so contented
As I feel with you.

Little spotted calf
Frolicking beside her mother,
Flag of a tail flicking the air,
Rear hooves flinging drops of dew
As she spins her morning circles-
Could she possibly be as secure
As I feel with you?

Sylvia Cook Bright
Copyright

COULD HAVE

He could have declined
To come from His throne,
Minister to me
When I was alone;

But He didn't.

You, too, could have said,
"I can't get involved
With all those problems
And pains unresolved;"

But you didn't.

For friends don't refuse
To help when they can.
They finish the work
My First Friend began.

Sylvia Cook Bright
Copyright 1985

FEELING FRAGMENTED?

Feeling fragmented?

Are you sure your shattered shell

Is broken beyond repair?

Be reminded, remember:

The Father, Who knows you well,

Gives no more than you can bear.

Sylvia Cook Bright
Copyright 1985

HEBREWS 13:8

The months march past
And we turn the calendar page.
This year will be the last
That we will be this age.

The seconds sweep
On the clock's expressionless face.
The vault is set to keep
Our treasures in their place.

We've named the days
As if to keep each week the same,
But sun and sundial play
A changing kind of game.

This decade's done.
We'd face the future insecure
If there were not One
Of Whom we could be sure;

But we have heard
The news the world was waiting for:
"Jesus the changeless Word,
Today and evermore!"

Sylvia Cook Bright
Copyright 1986

REMEMBER ME

Initials
Carved on a tree
Are crying out,
"Remember me."

Bent postcards
Tied with a cord
Were memorized,
Lovingly stored.

A helmet,
A bayonet,
Beg us, "Oh please,
Do not forget."

The scrapbook,
Yellowed with age,
Lets memories
Speak from each page.

So, I too,
Join the refrain:
Remember me,
We'll meet again.

Sylvia Cook Bright
Copyright 15 August 1984

NO STRINGS

YOU'RE HELPING ME BECOME

WHATEVER I'M GOING TO BE.

YOUR FRIENDSHIP HAS NO STRINGS;

I'M FREE JUST TO BE ME.

YOU'RE WAITING HERE WITH ME

FOR WHATEVER'S AROUND THE BEND.

I'M SO VERY THANKFUL

TO HAVE YOU FOR MY FRIEND.

Sylvia Cook Bright
Copyright 1985

OPPRESSED

The sky is oppressive today,
Seeming unable to bear its own weight;
So it hovers precariously,
About to precipitate,
And threatens to give way.

A fear that long has been suppressed,
Lurking, crouching, is ready to spring.
There it waits to devour me.
My mind is the plaything
Of feelings unexpressed.

With pressures I can't comprehend,
Smothered and driven, today is the day
I'd lose touch with reality,
If God in His knowing way
Had never sent a FRIEND.

Sylvia Cook
Copyright 10 May 1968

PEACE

My eyes are closed in peace,
Not death,
Just peace.
My mind has found release
In death,
Such peace.

The grave won't hold me long.
He comes!
Oh peace.
My death has turned to song.
I've found
My peace.

This body soon is gone.
It knows
No peace.
My soul is at the Dawn.
Praise God
For peace.

Such peace and without pain.
So free
This peace.
I've left to rise again.
Don't cry.
Here's peace.

Sylvia Cook
Copyright 15 January 1958

TIMELESSNESS OF LOVE

The snowflakes from a thousand mountains
Are crystal flowing streams.
The waters in the Incan fountains
Have dried, the mortar steams.
Yet nothing checks the passage
Of all my precious dreams.

From temples that were dark and thickened
A hint of gray looks down.
All the leaves that from buds were quickened
Are painted gold and brown.
But still I wear your mem'ry
Untarnished, as a crown.

A diamond that was in the forming
When first you touched my face
Was shattered by volcanic warming
In some forgotten place,
While not a single gesture
I'm able to erase.

The decades and eons and ages,
A minute and a span,
Are a book with its wordless pages
Blown by a summer fan.
It seems that I have loved you
Since time itself began.

Sylvia Bright

REPRIEVE

Dusty road before me,
Long's the path I've trod.
Is there any resting?
Is there any God?

Oh, my feet are weary,
The dust is choking me.
Rocks and stones are piercing,
No sign of rest I see.

Is that rain before me?
Oh, the hope of rest!
Could I feel that dampness?
Could I be so blessed?

Dusty road before me,
Throat so parched and dry
Oh! The rain is coming!
Look! There in the sky!

Such a blessed feeling:
God, such hope I've gained,
For just two steps before me,
Praise God! It's rained!

Sylvia Cook
Copyright 29 July 1958

SERENITY

Any serene, green valley
In North Georgia or Tennessee
Speaks with eloquent silence
Of the peace created to be.

The Creator Who is greater
Than the oppressor within me,
Can calm chaotic violence,
And set me peacefully free.

To stand on Carolina sand,
To feel the warm wind's caress,
Is to reaffirm, rehearse,
The Creator's worthiness.

From this, depression's abyss,
His hands lift with tenderness.
Thus, the Lord of the universe
Is the Master of my distress.

Sylvia Cook Bright
Copyright 19 July 1984

THE BOY AT THE BEACH

The boy at the beach, skipping stones,
Knows nothing of concentric theories.
It's his nature to notice the ripples and rings,
Unaware that the waves are in series.

My friend breaks my surface tension
With love, but would hardly suspect
How deeply I'm stirred, eternally changed,
Never knowing friendships' final effect.

Sylvia Cook Bright
Copyright 1981

THE CHRYSALIS

Your laughter envelopes me;
It is a safe cocoon
Spun around me,
Tailored to my need.

Your friendship is my growing place.
I realized so soon
After meeting you
That I'd been changed, indeed.

Your hand covering mine, forms
A golden chrysalis,
Sheltering me
While old becomes new.

Snug inside your encouragement,
My metamorphosis
Begins; I emerge
A better person, through you.

Sylvia Cook Bright
Copyright 9 June 1984

TO WHOM SHALL I
GO HOME NOW?

To whom shall I go home now?
The folks are dead and gone;
Their house is just a chimney
And weeds have choked the lawn.

With sisters, brothers, cousins
In towns and distant lands,
I've nothing left to hold now
But these tiny, little hands.

Ah, these tiny, little hands
And sleepy eyes, what do they see?
All too soon my own dear children
Will be coming home to me.

Sylvia Cook Bright
Copyright 1979

THE STEPPING STONE

Trying to cross this stream, I must reach the other side;
But wherever I put my foot, I only slip and slide.
Ah, there's the stone I seek, centered so, between the banks.
For a rock that is high and dry, I gladly give my thanks.
Praise to the Creator of slippery stones and dry.
Just when I needed, He heeded; He heard before my cry.

Catastrophic crises mingle with stresses and strain.
All the while this hectic lifestyle inflicts increasing pain.
Ah, I am not alone, for friendship is sent to calm:
In wilderness, an oasis, in anguish, soothing balm.
Praise to the Creator of friendships like yours and mine,
As they most certainly must be part of the Grand Design.

Sylvia Cook Bright
Copyright 1983

TOMORROW COMES

Tomorrow comes.
And though we cringe with fear,
Much the same as days before, a new day will appear.
Tomorrow comes,
Comes changing night to day.
Though we know not what lies in store, tomorrow comes our way.

Tomorrow comes.
And though this hour is dear,
Though we hold fast to this breath, another day is near.
Tomorrow comes,
Seems merciless and cold.
For all of life and all of death lies helpless in its hold.

Tomorrow comes.
It comes in darkest night.
When seems our life is spent, then comes the dawn and light.
Tomorrow comes.
Its sun dispels the gloom.
Fears and cares of night are sent. It opens night's cold tomb.

Tomorrow comes.
He said to watch and pray.
He may come at night or morn. Tomorrow is the day!
Tomorrow comes
Til glory fills the skies.
With this promise we are born: Tomorrow comes! We rise!

Sylvia Cook
Copyright 1960

WHISPERS

In the fragrant pine forest,
Georgia needles cushion my feet.
All alone, I hear a whisper,
Soft and low and sweet.

Though the wind is resting,
The sound is one I know;
The gentle, whispered memory
Of a friend from long ago.

On the maddening freeway,
Bombarded by sights and noise,
I'm comforted by a familiar whisper
Of remembered laughter and joys.

Splashing at the seashore
With sandpipers squawking at gulls,
What is that faintest whisper
That soothes and calms and lulls?

My friend is here beside me
As my memory soars through the past,
And I welcome the whispered reminder
Of a friendship that will always last.

Sylvia Cook Bright
Copyright 22 April 1984

WORDS

Crimson words
Appalachian sassafras in fall
Fluffy words
Kittens curled into a fuzzy ball

Splashing words
Water crashing over mountain rocks
PenT-up words
Rings of rusty keys to long-lost locks

Lightning words
Storm-sent shorthand spelled in Zs and Ys
Twinkling words
The dotted Swiss of stars in August skies

Timely words
Tulips braving February's freeze
Billowed words
Cloud-clowns changing costumes in the breeze

I need words
To let you know how much you mean to me
Written words
Print on pages penned for you to see

Praising words
Saying, Thanks, and I admire you.
Pleading words
Ask, Please forgive the ugly things I do.

Without words
What other way would I have to choose?
What are words?
To speak my thoughts, they're all I have to use.

Sylvia Cook Bright
Copyright 28 November 1985

YOUR GRACE IS SUFFICIENT
II Corinthians 12:9

Through the searing pain of separation,
The embarrassment of defeat,
When others cry in desperation,
Or try to hide behind deceit,

Though stretched to the limit of endurance,
With the way ahead so hard to see,
I calmly rest in words of assurance:
Your grace is sufficient for me.

Thus may I ever understand clearly,
As disappointing as life can be:
I have a Father Who loves me dearly,
Whose grace is sufficient for me.

Sylvia Cook Bright
Copyright 1986

A LESSON

THE FIRST TIME YOUR LITTLE HAND CLASPED AROUND
MY FINGER,
I LEARNED A LESSON IN TRUST.
SOMETIMES I WOULD STAND, AND BY YOUR CRADLE
LINGER,
AS IF LINGER I MUST.

THE DAY YOU LEARNED TO WALK, WHO
WAS PROUDER, YOU OR I?
HOW I'VE ENJOYED WATCHING YOU
GROW!
WHEN YOU BEGAN TO TALK, AND THE DAYS BEGAN TO
FLY,
I LEARNED A LESSON OF LOVE, I KNOW.

Sylvia Cook Bright
Copyright 1 May 1986

www.ingramcontent.com/pod-product-compliance
Lightning Source LLC
Chambersburg PA
CBHW042058030726
47602CB00004B/63